New Mexico Hot Springs Guide

By
Rick Cahill

PRUETT **P** PUBLISHING COMPANY
Boulder, Colorado

Library of Congress Cataloging-in-Publication Data

Cahill, Rick, 1950–
    New Mexico hot springs guide.

    Bibliography: p.
    Includes indexes.
    1. Hot springs—New Mexico. I. Title.
GB1198.3.N6C34 1988   917.89C453   88-9882
ISBN 0-87108-750-2

First Edition
2 3 4 5 6 7 8 9

Disclaimer

It is advisable to check with local or state authorities regarding access and sanitary condition of hot springs.

Acknowledgments

Many thanks to all the people who assisted in making the **New Mexico Hot Spring Guide** as complete as it is. I am especially grateful to Val Kurapka for driving those lonely roads and Carrie Carson for typing the final manuscript. My thanks also to the Truth or Consequences Historical Society, U.S. Geological Survey and New Mexico Bureau of Mines & Mineral Resources for contributing valuable photos and information. And lastly, appreciation is due my publisher for taking interest in my esoteric projects.

Author's Note

Your comments and suggestions to make **New Mexico Hot Spring Guide** more useful are highly valued. If you find something new or discontinued, let us know so we can include it in our next edition. All contributions (maps, photos and letters) will be saved and acknowledged. If we use your photos or maps, you will be mentioned in the credits. The publisher, however, is not responsible for unsolicited materials and cannot return them. Send only good quality black-and-white or color prints. Pruett Publishing will own publication rights to all material submitted.

Rick Cahill
c/o Pruett Publishing Company
2928 Pearl Street
Boulder, CO 80301

NEW MEXICO HOT SPRINGS

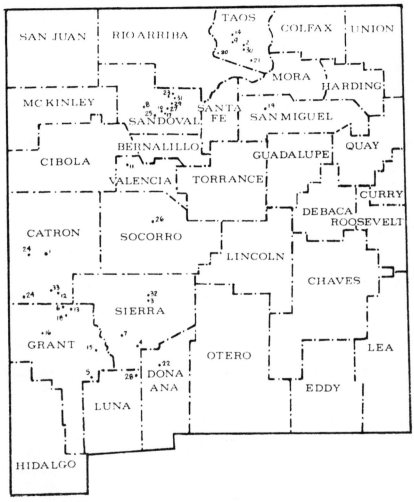

1. Aragon	12. Lightfeather	23. San Antonio
2. Black Rock	13. Lyons Hunting Lodge	24. San Francisco
3. Charles Bathhouse	14. Mamby's	25. San Ysidro
4. Derry Warm Spg.	15. Mimbres	26. Socorro
5. Faywood	16. Mangas	27. Soda Dam
6. Gila Springs	17. McCauley	28. Souse
7. Hilsbro	18. Melanie	29. Spence
8. Indian	19. Montezuma	30. Stagecoach
9. Hondo	20. Ojo Caliente	31. Sulphur
10. Jemez	21. Ponce de Leon	32. Truth or Consequences
11. Laguna Pueblo	22. Radium	33. Upper Middle Fork

iv

Contents

Introduction   ix

Precautions   xi

How to Use This Guide   xii

Maps   xiii

Catron County

San Francisco Hot Springs (Lower)   1

San Francisco Hot Springs (Upper)   4

Frisco Box Canyon Spring   7

Dona Ana County

Radium Springs   11

Grant County

Faywood Hot Springs   15

Gila Hot Springs Center   19

Lightfeather Hot Spring   25

Lyons Hunting Lodge Springs   28

Melanie Hot Spring   29

Turkey Creek Hot Springs   31

Upper Middle Fork Hot Spring   33

Sandoval County

Battleship Rock Hot Spring 35

Jemez Springs 39

    Soda Dam 42

San Antonio Hot Springs 45

San Ysidro Hot Springs 45

Spense Hot Springs 51

San Miguel County

Montezuma Hot Springs 55

Sierra County

Truth or Consequences 59

    Yucca Garden Lodge 61

    Charles Bathhouse 63

    Artesian Bathhouse and Trailer Court 64

    Marshall Apartments 65

    Dave's Cloverleaf Baths 65

    Ye Old Hot Spring Bath Haus 67

Collins Place 67

Indian Springs Apartments 67

Royce Baths 68

Brooks Apartments and Bathhouse 68

Ace Lodge 68

Socorro County

Socorro Hot Springs 71

Taos County

Hondo/Blackrock Hot Springs 73

Ojo Caliente Hot Springs 77

Ponce de Leon Hot Springs 81

Stagecoach Hot Springs 95

Minerals and Nutrition 86

Alphabetical Index 89

Map Index 90

HOT SPRING DIAGRAM

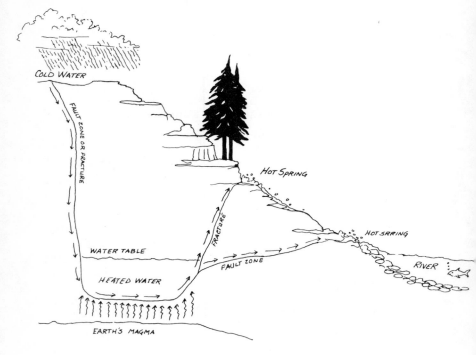

COLD WATER

FAULT ZONE OR FRACTURE

WATER TABLE

HEATED WATER

EARTH'S MAGMA

FRACTURE

FAULT ZONE

HOT SPRING

HOT SPRING

RIVER

Introduction

Every so often I get the urge to get away from it all, to get lost in the wilderness, to be alone to reflect and meditate. When this urge strikes, I know it's time to go exploring for hot springs. Hot spring hopping is a state of mind more than anything else. It's an excuse to get out of town and into the wilderness; it's a chance to slow down and take a closer look at the natural world in which we live, to study geology and geography, to learn about ancient Indian tribes and archaeology, to appreciate the flora and fauna of the countryside. People who visit hot springs enjoy exploration, and the search is often more satisfying than the end result.

The American Indians knew the secret power of natural hot waters, for it was here that they believed the "Great Spirit" lived. To them hot springs were sacred places where broken bodies were healed, as well as broken spirits. Perhaps these Indians had the right idea, and in my own way I, too, believe hot springs are sacred, especially wilderness springs. There is something about them that gives me an understanding of my place in the universe. There's also some- thing romantic and exciting about exploring areas that were once inhabited by ancient people. At the nearby hot springs it's not terribly difficult to imagine an ancient Anasazi making the trek from his cliff palace apartment to cleanse his spirit and ease his aches in a ritual bath of healing water.

Half the fun of writing a book on hot springs is the exploration. Driving around in wilderness areas and seeing some of the most beautiful geography in the nation could hardly be considered work. But, at times, the search can be rather frustrating. I set off on many wild goose chases.

Inaccurate maps and sketchy information were just a few of my problems; harsh weather conditions, private ownership, and the shear remote locality of some springs added to my frustration. In my search for the best hot springs in New Mexico I was often disappointed, and at one point I was going to abandon the project. It was just too depressing to see what had become of some of these natural wonders. Some had been bulldozed, others had been dynamited, still others had been neglected and vandalized to the point of no return. But we continued searching, hoping that our research would reveal a brighter picture. Although we located plenty of springs to compile a book, the future of these thermal areas is uncertain.

The springs compiled in this book will provide you with an excellent sampling of the hot springs that are left in New Mexico. Come with us as we hike miles into the remote mountain wilderness and explore deep river canyons in our quest for the best hot springs in the west.

Precautions

The following is a list of the most common precautions and hazards that you might encounter on your hot spring explorations. Go prepared and beware of all potential dangers.

Always carry water.

Take appropriate clothing. During the summer wear a wide-brimmed hat. Always carry extra clothing in case the weather should take a turn for the worse. Wear gear appropriate to the type of terrain you'll be hiking.

Beware of snakes. There are eleven species of rattlesnake in New Mexico. The coral snake and gila monster are two more good reasons to watch your footing. Winter is the safest time of year to hike in the desert, a time when most snakes are in hybernation.

The scorpion and the black widow spider are just two of the poisonous arthropods you might encounter in New Mexico. Know what they look like.

Carry a first aid kit.

Be familiar with the symptoms of hypothermia and heat exhaustion; know first aid treatment for both.

To keep from getting lost, stay on established trails.

Always carry a flashlight, matches and compass.

Always check with a forest ranger before embarking on any long wilderness hike.

Know your limit. Make sure you're in shape before attempting long strenuous hikes.

Don't hike alone, if possible.

Be aware of weather conditions.

Those with high blood pressure and heart conditions should consult with a physician before using hot springs.

How to Use This Guide

This guide is designed to help you locate hot springs easily and quickly. It contains an overall map of New Mexico showing where hot springs are located in the state. You can then look up the springs in the table of contents which is alphabetically arranged by county. This structure is intended to provide the reader with information on hot springs in the same general area. For your convenience we've also included an alphabetical index of all the hot springs at the back of the book.

At the beginning of each hot spring listing there are vital statistics: name, location, elevation, temperature, flow and services. A composite map and general description is furnished for each individual spring.

This book is a compilation of information gleaned from several state and federal agencies; however, through my research, I found that this information is not always correct. For instance in some publications springs have been double listed under different ames, others are inaccurately described and located. The springs in this book have all been field-checked and the names are the most commonly used.

Maps

On the overall map of New Mexico we've listed almost every hot spring known. The text doesn't comment on all, simply because some are located on private property, others aren't worth the trip, and a few are just too remote. Yet their approximate locations are marked on the map for those who enjoy a challenge and knowing they've taken a path less traveled. The composite maps are nothing more than simple field sketches. They are not drawn to scale, and the directional arrow is approximate. U.S. geological survey topographical maps are available for most of these areas. These maps are helpful for locating specific topographical features and will ultimately add to your hot spring experience.

SAN FRANCISCO HOT SPRINGS

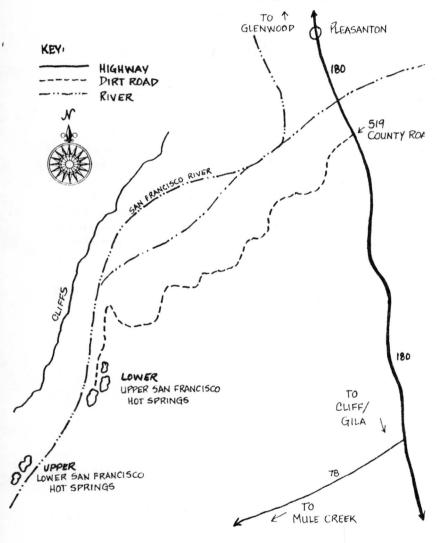

KEY:
— HIGHWAY
----- DIRT ROAD
-·-·- RIVER

N

TO GLENWOOD ↑   PLEASANTON

180

← 519 COUNTY ROAD

SAN FRANCISCO RIVER

CLIFFS

LOWER
UPPER SAN FRANCISCO
HOT SPRINGS

180

TO CLIFF/GILA ↓

UPPER
LOWER SAN FRANCISCO
HOT SPRINGS

78

TO ← MULE CREEK

San Francisco Hot Springs—Lower (Catron County)

Location: There are two groups of hot springs in this area: Upper San Francisco Hot Springs and Lower San Francisco Hot Springs. Located in the Apache National Forest, about one and a half miles south of Pleasanton, New Mexico, just off Highway 180. Take a dirt road marked 519 to the right and follow it all the way to the end. The lower springs are located on the east bank of the San Francisco River while the upper springs are located about one-third mile upstream from the lower springs on the west bank.

Elevation: 4600 feet

Temperature: 121°F (49°C)

Flow: 37 gpm

Services: Restrooms

We were looking for a spring we'd never seen, in a place we'd never been. Not only had someone taken the sign down on Highway 180, the directions we had were sketcky and inaccurate. After two unsuccessful hiking attempts, we started out on a third, and just as the sun was setting, we hoped that this was the right road to the elusive springs. Driving up the rutted road, which was cut into the steep canyon wall high above the river, we searched for any signs of hot spring activity.

As we bounced along we discussed what we might find at the springs. Would this be a quiet place to visit with few

1

Young children channel water from the lower San Francisco Hot Springs into the river.—*Author's Photo*

people? Would the springs be clean and usable or would they be neglected or even destroyed like so many other springs we had visited?

After a mile or so, the road led down to an open parking area filled with campers, pickups and cars. The bustling activity around the springs was a startling contrast to the quiet countryside. Campfires were already blazing, fishermen were pulling in their lines and a few people were taking their last soak of the day by the river's edge.

Although hot water issues from several spots along the river bank, there are only two shallow pools used for soaking. Even though there were quite a few people visiting the springs, no one seemed to mind and everyone took their turn.

But that was back in 1986. Since then something disturbing has happened.

We returned in the summer of 1987 only to find warning notices posted. This is what we read:

Warning. Tests performed at the New Mexico State Health and Environment Department Laboratory Division confirmed the presence of an amoeba in the waters of San Francisco Hot Springs. This amoeba, (naegbria fowleri) causes meningo-encephalitis, an infection of the brain. The amoeba enters the human body through the nose and migrates to the brain leading to coma and death. Although this form of meningitis is rare, the public should avoid the risk of contracting this disease by not bathing in the hot springs in this area. Symptoms of the disease may be a runny nose or sore throat, followed by severe headache. Parents of healthy children and young adults who have been bathing in those waters and have the described symptoms should immediately contact their physician.

For further information contact the State of New Mexico Health and Environment Department, Santa Fe, New Mexico.

Although warnings are posted, hot spring lovers still flock to the Lower San Francisco Hot Springs. Some just come to soak their tired feet, while others ignore the signs and take the risk of bathing in the warm waters. Still others come simply because it's a beautiful place to camp and relax. The springs may be a little disappointing, but the fishing is good and the scenery is even better.

The nearest services are a few miles north in the town of Pleasanton. On your way you'll find a historic marker dedicated to the memory of Aldo Leopold, a forester and ecologist who helped establish the first national forest: the Gila Wilderness. From this vantage point you'll be able to point out Outlaw Mountain, Saddle Mountain, Lookout Ridge, Haystack Mountain, Glenwood Brushy and Sheridan Gulch.

Another group of hot springs are located about one-half mile downstream from the lower springs on the west bank of the river. Here you'll find hot water discharging from the river's edge at several different spots.

About six miles north is the town of Glenwood. The Blue Front Bar/Cafe is about the only place in town where you can wet your whistle and get a bite to eat. Although the restaurant doesn't open up until 5:00 P.M., the bar stocks pickled eggs and Louisiana Red Hots (a pickled beef and pork product) to tide you over.

Nearby, a popular attraction called the Catwalk draws tourists from all over the nation to see a historic pipeline that was built to bring water to the silver mill. The pipe is fastened to sheer canyon walls, and the men who once worked on it had to have the surefootedness of a cat. Today anyone can walk the pipeline, since a metal fence encloses the catwalk, and experience cascading waterfalls, quiet pools and glimpse into the deep canyon that only receives light at midday.

San Francisco Hot Springs (Upper)—*Author's Photo*

San Francisco Hot Springs—Upper

Location: Located along the west bank of the San Francisco River about ten miles north of Pleasanton on Highway 180.

Elevation: 4600 feet

Temperature: 90°F (37°C)

Flow: 6.9 gpm

Services: None

Along the west bank of the San Francisco River, a series of steaming hot springs bubble peacefully. To reach the upper springs, cross the river at the parking area at the Lower San Francisco Hot Springs and hike south. You'll cross the river three times; however, if is low water season you can hike the entire distance down the middle of the river. It's a refreshing summer trek.

When you arrive you'll find natural mineral water flowing from several different spots along the bank. Small soaking pools, at temperatures ranging from 90 to 100 degrees, are scattered down river.

Although this spring is located on National Forest land and is accessible all year (except high water season), it is recommended that you check with the Forest Service regarding the sanitary condition of the springs.

This area of the Southwest offers several other unusual outdoor activities that aren't available to other regions of the United States. For instance you can take a llama or horsepack trip along the San Francisco River, or hike into the Mogollon Mountains. It's a colorful country with a history of silver mining, Apache attacks and cattle ranching. See Lower San Francisco Hot Springs.

Along the highway to the springs an official scenic historic marker gives information about the Mogollon Mountains. The sign reads: "The mountains and the town were named for Juan Ignacio Flores Mogollon, governor of New Mexico from 1712 to 1715. the name also applied to the Pueblo Indians who abandoned the area in the 1400s. These mountains were inhabited by the Apaches until the late 19th century."

FRISCO BOX CANYON
SPRING

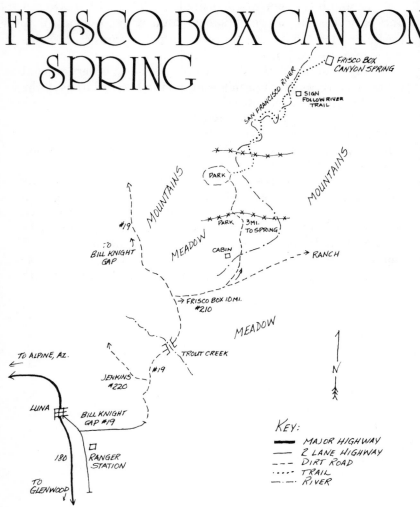

Frisco Box Canyon Spring (Catron County)

Location: Located approximately eight and one-half miles east of the ranger station at Luna, New Mexico, and approximately one and one-half miles up the San Francisco River.

Elevation: approximately 8200 feet

Temperature: 98°F (37°C)

Flow: 6.9 gpm

Services: None

If you're planning a trip to Frisco Box Hot Spring, you're in for one of the most beautiful hikes of your life. Located in the Apache National Forest, this wilderness hot tub is outstanding among New Mexico's watering places.

To reach the springs, travel 8 ½ miles east of the U.S. Forest Service Station at Luna. If you have difficulty finding it, the helpful folks at the Luna Mercantile will point you in the right direction.

Once you're on Bill Knight Gap Road, you'll pass through private land, so close the gate when entering and leaving. Be forewarned, it's a rough, suspension pounding journey, and when the road becomes too difficult to negotiate, it's time to get out of your car and walk. The springs are located another 1 ½ miles upstream, though it seems farther.

This is my favorite hot spring in New Mexico. Not only is it a challenge to locate, for you have to ford the river no less than seven times, but also the beauty of the area makes every step a joy. Yellow and red wildflowers carpet the banks of the

Ask at the Luna Mercantile, and they'll direct you to Frisco Box Canyon Hot Spring. *Author's Photo*

The trail to Frisco Box Hot Spring follows the river. —*Author's Photo*

river, and the sweet wind blows through the fragrant pines, energizing and revitalizing the spirit.

The canyon you're walking in cuts through the San Francisco Mountains and is known locally as "The Box." Although it sometimes seems as if you'll never find the springs, all you have to do is follow the San Francisco River and eventually you'll stumble across a concrete tub located about forty feet above the bed of the river.

At last you can soothe your aching body in a steaming wilderness bath. The long hike was worth it. From here you have a spectacular view of the river below and the surrounding San Francisco Mountains.

RADIUM SPRINGS

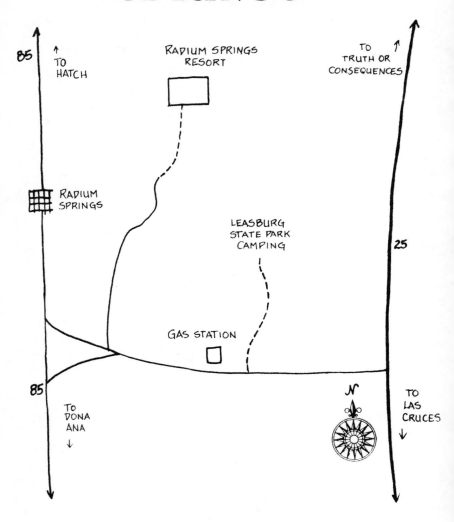

85

TO
HATCH

TO
TRUTH OR
CONSEQUENCES

RADIUM SPRINGS
RESORT

RADIUM
SPRINGS

LEASBURG
STATE PARK
CAMPING

25

GAS STATION

85

TO
DONA
ANA

N

TO
LAS
CRUCES

Radium Springs (Dona Ana County)

Location: Located in the town of Radium Springs northwest of Las Cruces, New Mexico on Highway 85.

Elevation: 4000 feet

Temperature: 142°F (61°C)

Flow: No flow. Water pumped.

Services: Swimming pool, individual hot tubs, steam baths and massage, restaurant, lodging, and camping. Open all year.

According to the hotel's brochure the history of the Radium Springs Resort is rather colorful.

At the turn of the century a Harvey House was built near the springs to serve the travelers on the Santa Fe Railway. Supposedly, in 1931 Harry Bailey, a friend of Pat Garret and Billy the Kid, built a hotel and bathhouse so that visitors could have access to the refreshing waters once known as Seldon Springs. Back then it was advertised as Bailey's Baths.

But it hasn't been all glory and glamor. In fact, from 1978–1982 the hotel was leased to the state of New Mexico and used as a women's prison. The stark furnishings in one of the wings reflects its former use. Wrought iron bars still blocked a few windows.

Today the resort is making a comeback. The present owner, former dentist Bill Daly, is steadily improving the property. He bought the resort from his parents, who had owned it since 1966, and has set up a gourmet restaurant, called Yesterdays, which serves Hungarian food.

Reproduction of a 1931 brochure advertising the new hotel at
Radium Springs.—*Courtesy Radium Springs Hotel*

At the turn of the century Radium Springs was a popular stop on the Santa Fe Railroad and the site of a Harvey House.—*Author's Photo*

Bill has plans of renovating the swimming pool with separate bathhouses for men and women on either side. And just off the main dining room he plans to use a quiet, shady patio for outdoor dining and barbeques.

There are also other diversions in the area like shopping in nearby Juarez, Mexico, hunting in the Organ Mountains, fishing and boating on Elephant Butte Lake and picnicking and hiking in the White Sands National Monument.

All in all, this is a quaint little resort that is located off the beaten path along the Rio Grande River.

For more information contact:

Radium Springs Resort
P.O. Box 35
Radium Springs, NM 88054

or call

505-524-4093

FAYWOOD HOT SPRINGS

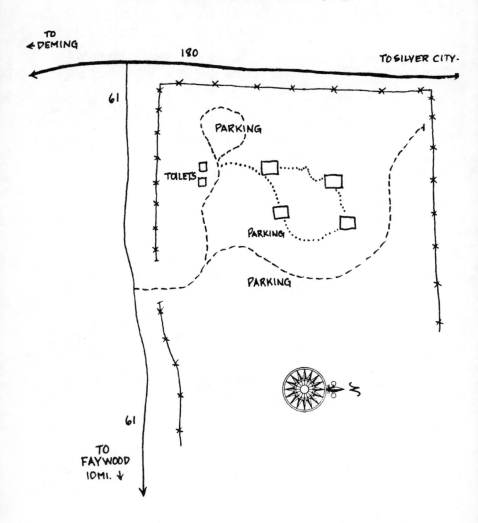

Faywood Hot Springs (Grant County)

Location: Located south of Silver City, New Mexico on Highway 61 about a mile past the City of Rocks State Park in Kennecott Copper Mining property. Traveling east, turn left off the highway onto dirt road. Four pools filled with mineral water. Overnight parking permitted. Grant County.

Elevation: 4000 feet

Temperature: 129°F (54°C)

Flow: 100 gpm

Services: None.

Faywood Hot Springs was a nice place to visit in 1986, but since then something has happened. Health notices have been posted warning curious travelers about the dangers of trespassing, and the owners, Kennecott Mining Company, have had the entrance bulldozed in an attempt to deter hot spring lovers.

The four pools, which now stand neglected, are under seige by swarms of horseflies. The outhouses sit crooked on their foundations, doors wide open, but no one is around to notice. The campsites are vacant and broken picnic tables are lonely monuments to a once popular bathing spot.

The sparse vegetation of this high desert area (wolfberry, salt brush and quail sage) is contrasted by the springs' thickly overgrown tall grasses. Honeycomb trails once led you to four individual, concrete-lined pools filled with natural mineral water that constantly flows from a main spring at the top of

Young children frolic around the edge of a crude hot tub at Faywood.—*Author's Photo*

the hill. People once came here to this little oasis to camp and enjoy the soothing springs, but something has happened and now only the flies are left.

I camped here in 1986 and recall it as one of the most pleasant experiences of my summer. Everywhere you could see evidence of the joy of hot springs; children and adults soaking in the warm waters, laughing and having fun.

I was in for a shocking surprise when I visited again in the summer of 1987. It was as though the area had been hit by some sort of terrible plague. What happened to this beautiful oasis? I wondered. Perhaps it was the lack of sanitary facilities that caused the decline of the condition of the springs, or perhaps vandals trashed them. In any case, it was a depressing sight.

Maybe one day some energetic entreprenuer will purchase the springs, clean them up, and restore them. Then again perhaps Faywood will be forgotten forever. No one knows for sure.

It's a shame to witness the destruction of a natural wonder such as Faywood Hot Springs, for it has been with us for a long time. Geologists and hydrologists have been writing about Faywood for more than a hundred years, and its history goes back millions of years. Situated within a mile of the Blue Mountain Fault, the hot springs bubble up through volcanic gravels formed during the Paleozoic period.

Just down the road you can camp at the City of Rocks State Park where you'll see huge boulders rising some fifty or sixty feet in the air. It is said that these ancient rhyolite outcroppings were once a favorite lookout for Apaches waiting to ambush stagecoaches on the Butterfield Trail. Campsites are set among the rocks, sheltering you from the high desert wind. You'll also find a botanical garden in one part of the park that features some of the Southwest's unusual plantlife; especially beautiful in the springtime when the cactus are blooming.

About twenty-five miles north is Silver City, a town born of the silver boom back in 1870, where you'll find motels and restaurants. This is the largest town in this part of the state and is a good place to stock up on supplies before heading further north into the Gila Wilderness Area, another area renown for its thermal activity.

GILA RIVER BASIN AREA

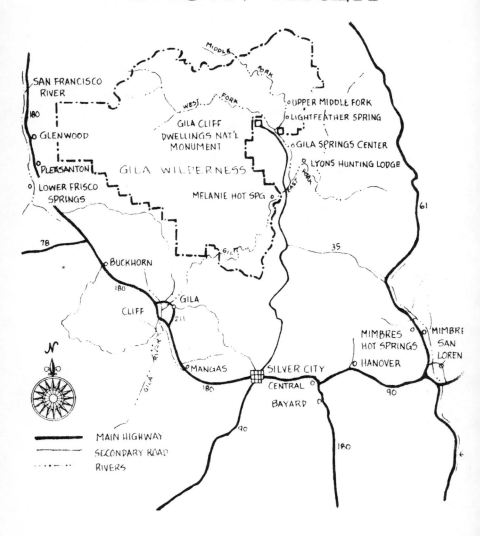

SAN FRANCISCO RIVER

180

GLENWOOD

PLEASANTON

LOWER FRISCO SPRINGS

78

BUCKHORN

180

CLIFF

GILA

211

MANGAS

180

MIDDLE FORK

WEST FORK

GILA CLIFF DWELLINGS NAT'L MONUMENT

GILA WILDERNESS

MELANIE HOT SPG

GILA

UPPER MIDDLE FORK

LIGHTFEATHER SPRING

GILA SPRINGS CENTER

LYONS HUNTING LODGE

61

35

MIMBRES HOT SPRINGS

HANOVER

SILVER CITY
CENTRAL
BAYARD

90

90

180

MIMBRE SAN LOREN

N

MAIN HIGHWAY
SECONDARY ROAD
RIVERS

Gila Hot Springs Center (Grant County)

Location: Located north of Silver City and four miles below the Gila Cliff Dwellings National Monument on Highway 15. The road is not plowed on weekends or evenings. Caution for trailers over twenty feet, the road is steep, narrow and has many sharp curves. An alternate route Highway 90 to 35, a less treacherous drive, but not as scenic.

Elevation: Approximately 6000 feet

Temperature: 151°F (66°C)

Flow: 151 gpm

Services: Camping, picnic, RV spaces with hookups, lodge (reservations only), general store, horseback riding, soaking tub and whirlpool.

Drive about forty-four miles north of Silver City, New Mexico, on Highway 15 and you'll find yourself surrounded by the tall pines of the Gila National Forest. The Gila River Basin Area has a multitude of hot springs that could keep the hot spring lover busy for a week or more.

One of the more popular spots for the motorist and camper is the Gila Hot Spring Vacation Center located in the tiny town of Gila Hot Springs. Although there is only a hot spring bathhouse available for the customers of the RV park and four-room lodge, the area provides many other diversions such as hunting, hiking, horseback riding and fishing.

The Gila Hot Springs are located on the north side of the Middle Fork of the Gila River and not only supply hot water to

19

Doc Campbell's Trading Post is located in the small town of Gila Hot Springs. —*Author's Photo*

the bathhouse and whirlpool, but a trading post, restaurant, a few surrounding buildings, and the owner's ranch. D.A. Campbell and his family were some of the first settlers in this wilderness and have owned and operated this vacation resort for many years.

There's plenty of recreation in this area known as the Mogollons, the name of the principle mountain range in the area. It is a land of rugged mountains and shear canyons, a wilderness that was once inhabited by the Apache Indians, and there's even evidence of an ancient tribe.

The Gila Cliff Dwellings National Monument, one of the earliest national monuments, has been protected since 1924. Located within the Gila Wilderness Area, one of the largest wildernesses in the nation, these dwellings are surrounded by ponderosa pine and are one of the most popular attractions.

These cliff dwellings were built by Indians in the thirteenth and fourteenth centuries and provide spectacular views of their ancient way of life. The visitor's center, located three miles north of the town of Gila Hot Springs, displays artifacts and sells books and maps of the area. The rangers are

Not far from Gila Hot Springs ancient Anasazi cliff dwellings offer an interesting diversion.—*Author's Photo*

always happy to point out the numerous trails in the park, and some of these trails lead to hot springs (See Lightfeather and Upper Middle Fork).

The Gila visitor center is open from 8:00 A.M. to 5:00 P.M. daily. Interpretive talks are given every Saturday night, Memorial Day through Labor Day, by cliff dwellings personnel.

The Gila Cliff Dwellings are open year-round, and visiting hours vary from season to season. It is recommended that visitors contact the Gila visitor center at 1-505-536-9461

You'll find a quiet RV resort and bathhouse in Gila Hot Springs.—
Author's Photo

to obtain current information on hours of operation. It takes
about one hour to walk the one-mile, self-guided loop trail to
the dwellings. Pets are not allowed in the monument, and
unlocked kennels are provided. Visitors may wish to bring a
padlock to use on the kennels for additional protection. Both
the visitor center and the Cliff Dwellings are closed on
Christmas Day and New Year's Day.

Developed and primitive campgrounds are available in
the Gila River Recreation Area. The Upper and Lower
Scorpion campgrounds, located about one-quarter mile from
the Cliff Dwellings parking area, have seventeen
camping/picnicking units with tables, grills and fireplaces at
each site. Drinking water and restrooms with sinks and flush
toilets are available during the warm months (approximately
May through September) when there is no danger of the pipes
freezing. Water can be obtained year-round at the visitor
center. A trailer dump station is situated at the junction of
Highway 15 and the spur road which leads to the Gila Cliff
Dwellings and Scorpion campground.

The Forks and Grapevine camping areas, six miles south of the visitor center, have twenty-five undeveloped sites. No water is available at either area, and vault toilets are the only restroom facilities at these locations.

Visitors can stable horses and pack animals at the public corral (T.J. Corral) located near the Scorpion campground. Horses are not allowed in any campground or the Cliff Dwellings area.

The nearest conventional overnight accommodations and restaurants are in Silver City. Groceries, snacks, soft drinks, camping and picnicking supplies, ice, and gasoline can be purchased at the store at Gila Hot Springs.

The surrounding Gila Wilderness and National Forest offer unlimited recreational opportunities for those who enjoy the outdoors. Mule deer, whitetail deer, elk, black bear, turkey, squirrel, dove, quail and other game species await the nature enthusiast. Rainbow trout are stocked periodically by the New Mexico Department of Game and Fish. The area stocked normally includes the West Fork of the Gila River from the Cliff Dwellings parking lot to the main Gila River bridge. Salmon eggs seem to be the most popular bait. Flies and spinners are used on the major streams in the Gila Wilderness. A state fishing license is required.

For more information contact:

Gila Hot Springs Vacation Center
HCR 88072
Gila Hot Springs
Silver City, NM 88061

or call

1-505-536-9551

GILA CLIFF DWELLINGS AREA

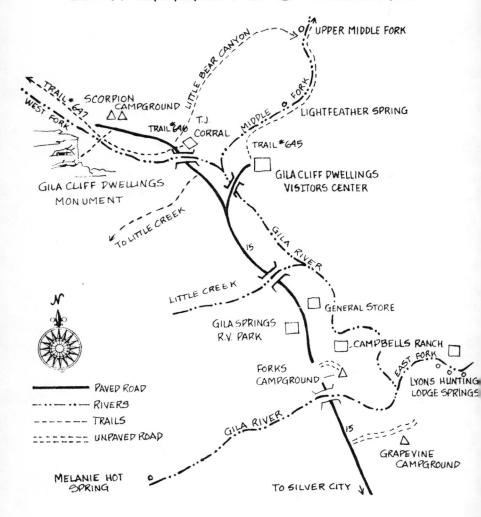

UPPER MIDDLE FORK

TRAIL #6A7

WEST FORK

SCORPION CAMPGROUND

LITTLE BEAR CANYON

MIDDLE FORK

LIGHTFEATHER SPRING

TRAIL #6A6

T.J. CORRAL

TRAIL #6A5

GILA CLIFF DWELLINGS MONUMENT

GILA CLIFF DWELLINGS VISITORS CENTER

TO LITTLE CREEK

15

GILA RIVER

LITTLE CREEK

GILA SPRINGS R.V. PARK

GENERAL STORE

CAMPBELLS RANCH

EAST FORK

N

FORKS CAMPGROUND

LYONS HUNTING LODGE SPRINGS

———— PAVED ROAD

—·—·— RIVERS

– – – – TRAILS

－－－－ UNPAVED ROAD

GILA RIVER

15

GRAPEVINE CAMPGROUND

MELANIE HOT SPRING

TO SILVER CITY

Lightfeather Hot Spring (Grant County)

Location: Located north from Silver City in the Gila Cliff Dwelling National Monument. From the visitor's center park and hike one-half mile up the middle fork of the Gila River to the spring.

Elevation: Approximately 8000 feet

Temperature: 150°F (53°C)

Flow: 47 gpm

Services: None.

The ranger told us to follow Trail Head No. 645 about one-half mile to a small spring. Bad weather loomed ahead of us as we started this hike up the middle fork of the Gila River, but we were confident that we could reach the spring, take our photographs and get out before the storm hit. We were in for a surprise.

It started as a moderate hike in which we climbed canyon walls and, losing the trail, were forced to ford the stream twice. For the most part the trail is up from the river.

No sooner had we arrived at the springs, which consist of four small pools, (largest being 6' X 6'), that issue from the base of a cliff, did thunderheads roll down the middle of the canyon. Lightning bolts flashed nearby, immediately followed by deafening claps of thunder. We scrambled up the side of the cliff where we took refuge in a cave overlooking the springs. We built a small fire at the mouth of the cave and decided to wait out the storm. We watched the storm for about an hour before it was safe to venture out.

A series of hot springs boil up along the shores of the West Fork of the
Gila River.—*Author's Photo*

This is one of the most interesting hot springs in New
Mexico. The trail conjures up ancient images, and one
wonders if this same trail was used by the Anasazi Indians in
the fourteenth century. Although no one knows for sure, it is
commonly accepted as historical fact that the Apache Indians
used the springs in the late 1800s. The rangers at the visitor
center will explain the history:

> Somewhere around the year 1885 the decaying
> remains of a "wicki-up" were discovered by the hot
> sulphur springs, which indicates that the springs were
> used as vapor baths for healing purposes. What is a
> "wicki-up?" It is a small hut, shaped somewhat like a

Springs issue at the base of a cliff.—*Author's Photo*

beehive, that was built over the springs. These shelters were made of willow branches which were embedded in the ground and bent in the form of a dome.

In the early morning light a white cloud of smoke rises up the steep slopes of the canyon. You wonder if you're seeing Indian smoke signals, but a closer look reveals that it is a warm steam from Lightfeather Hot Spring.

Lyons Hunting Lodge Springs
(Grant County)

Location: Located near the Gila Springs Center off Highway 15 north of Silver City, New Mexico.

Elevation: 6000 feet

Temperature: 126°F (52°C)

Flow: Piped

Services: Lodge. Reservation basis only.

Located in the remote Gila (hee-la) Wilderness, this spring is surrounded by the 3.3 million-acre Gila National Forest—one of the largest wilderness areas in the Rocky Mountains, and the first to be designated as such by congress in 1924.

Warm water issues at three places along the east fork of the Gila River, two of which are piped to the lodge swimming pool. The other is located a quarter mile or so up the canyon.

Although it's a little light on the hot springs, the East Fork Wilderness Ranch is the only resort in the area that accesses the thermal waters. This 750,000-acre ranch specializes in guided hunting, fishing and horsepacking tours. "My wife and I live in the lodge all year-round," says owner Gary Webb, "we like to maintain a homey-type atmosphere." Though April through November is the most popular time to visit, certain wildlife, including the American bald eagle, can only be viewed during the winter months.

For reservations or information on tours contact:

Gary and Julie Webb
Route 11, Box 75
Silver City, NM 88061

or call

1-505-536-9368

Melanie Hot Springs (Grant County)

Location: Located north of Silver City on Highway 15 where the Gila River runs under the highway. Park and take the trail south along the east bank of the main stem of Gila River. Be prepared for many river crossings. Spring issues about twenty to forty feet above river and cascades down rocks to the river.

Elevation: 5200 feet

Temperature: 112°F (44°C)

Flow: 20 gpm

Services: None. Check with the Forest Service.

A mile and a half south of Gila Hot Springs there's a bridge that crosses the river. Below it you'll find a camping area. This is a good place for a base camp if you're looking for these wilderness springs.

The serious hot spring explorer will find a delightful treat at the end of this sometimes treacherous hike along the Gila River. The trail crosses the river several times and appropriate shoes are recommended.

High waters make these springs difficult to reach during the rainy season. Any other time you'll find the springs bubbling to the surface twenty to forty feet above the cold, rushing river. The hot water cascades to a tranquil rock pool along the river's edge. Here, hikers languish under the open sky.

This is a spring for those who enjoy an afternoon of challenge. Take your fishing pole and catch yourself dinner on the way back to camp.

TURKEY CREEK SPRING

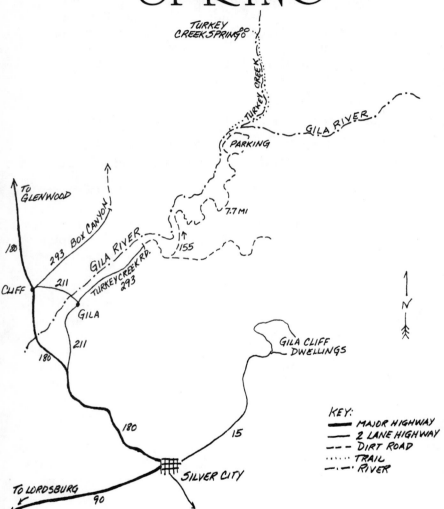

TURKEY CREEK SPRING

TURKEY CREEK

GILA RIVER

PARKING

TO GLENWOOD

293 BOX CANYON

GILA RIVER

7.7 MI

1155

180

211

TURKEY CREEK RD. 293

CLIFF

GILA

211

180

GILA CLIFF DWELLINGS

180

15

N

TO LORDSBURG

90

SILVER CITY

KEY:
— MAJOR HIGHWAY
— 2 LANE HIGHWAY
- - - DIRT ROAD
...... TRAIL
-·-·- RIVER

You have to ford Turkey Creek many times before you reach Turkey Creek Hot Springs.—*Author's Photo*

Turkey Creek Hot Springs (Grant County)

Location: Take Highway 180 to the Gila turnoff New Mexico State Highway 211. Go through town to NM 293 which eventually turns into Turkey Creek Road. From here it's another eight miles to a parking area. An eight mike hike will lead you to the springs.

Elevation: Approximately 8000 feet

Temperature: 183°F (74°C)

Flow: Unknown

Services: None.

The U.S. Geological Survey reported a hot spring somewhere along Turkey Creek. Although I knew it would be difficult to locate, I didn't think it would be the most difficult hike in this book. I was wrong.

Turkey Creek Road runs parallel to the Gila River for approximately eight bone-jarring miles and dead ends at a small parking area. From here we crossed the river to begin our hike, walking along the Gila until we came to the confluence of Turkey Creek. Then we followed the creek for several hours, but we had no idea how many miles it was to the spring, and everyone we met along the trail didn't know either. After five hours of searching we gave up and turned back.

On our return trip we came prepared with backpacks, sleeping bags and topographical map. Since we didn't begin hiking until around noon, we stayed the night in the wilderness.

It's approximately eight miles to the springs, and although they are the most pristine springs in the state, I only recommend them to the most diehard hot spring fanatics.

Upper Middle Fork Hot Spring
(Grant County)

Location: Located north from Silver City on Highway 15. Park at the T.J. Corral and take Trail Head No.646 up Little Bear Canyon about six miles to where the canyon and the middle fork merge. This is the shortest and driest route. Trail Head No.645 begins at the visitor's center. Check with the Forest Service before attempting this hike.

Elevation: 8500 feet

Temperature: Approximately 81°F (27°C)

Flow: 54 gpm

Services: None.

You have a choice in reaching this spring: wet or dry. The route mentioned above is the shortest and the driest. Another way to reach the spring is by taking Trail Head No.645 up to Lightfeather Hot Spring and continuing about six more miles to where Little Bear Canyon and the middle fork of the Gila merge. Continue another three miles downstream. The hot water discharges from multiple outlets on the northeast side of the river and flows over a rock-rubble slope. The water also boils up from the floor of the canyon.

Depending on which trail you take, be prepared to cross the river many times. Either route you choose will lead you to a secluded natural hot water pool with plenty of solitude—the scene conjures up images of Walden's Pond.

This is a good hike for a weekend camping trip and there is a hot bath as a reward for those who complete it.

Also in the area, further up the middle fork of the Gila about one-third mile upstream from Jordan Canyon (check topo map), is a small hot water seep called the Meadows, though it is not very popular with bathers.

SPENSE/
BATTLESHIP ROCK
HOT SPRINGS

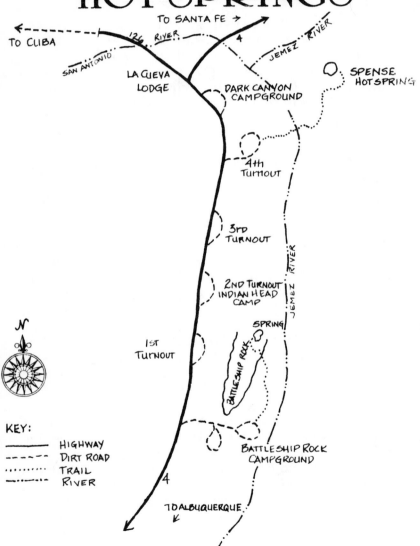

TO SANTA FE →

TO CUBA

126 RIVER

4

JEMEZ RIVER

SAN ANTONIO

LA CUEVA
LODGE

DARK CANYON
CAMPGROUND

SPENSE
HOTSPRING

4th
Turnout

3rd
Turnout

2nd Turnout
INDIAN HEAD
CAMP

JEMEZ RIVER

SPRING

1st
Turnout

BATTLESHIP ROCK

BATTLESHIP ROCK
CAMPGROUND

4

TO ALBUQUERQUE

N

KEY:

———— HIGHWAY
– – – – DIRT ROAD
·········· TRAIL
—·—·— RIVER

Battleship Rock Hot Spring
(Sandoval County)

Location: Located on the east fork of the Jemez River, five miles north of Jemez Pueblo on Highway 4. The spring is approximately one hundred feet above the river and one and one-tenth miles east of Battleship Rock in a camping area of same name. A tranquil mountain pool (about thirty by forty feet) is surrounded by lush foliage and tall pines.

Elevation: 7400 feet

Temperature: 90°F (32°C)

Flow: 368 gpm

Services: None.

Just down the road from Spense Hot Spring, Battleship Rock Hot Spring guarantees a scenic hike, and depending on which trail you take it can be a steep and strenuous exercise.

Start by taking the main trail, at the base of the rock. Follow the trail up the canyon, staying to the left when it branches. The idea is to go up the side of the mountain and away from the stream. After walking for an hour or so, you'll come to a clearing in the forest where you'll discover a natural pond (about thirty to forty feet in diameter and about three feet deep) filled with what appear to be thousands of tiny guppies. In the area you'll find two caves and several established campsites. And while overnight camping is okay, a sign at the entrance to the park says any cars left unattended for more than a twenty-four hour period will be towed at owner's expense.

There are established campsites and two caves at Battleship Rock Hot Spring.—*Author's Photo*

Battleship Rock Hot Spring is your reward for completing this two mile scenic hike.—*Author's Photo*

There is an alternate trail that leads to this serene hot spring. When you set out on your hike follow the Gila River until you come to a small rivulet (about a mile). The rivulet is run-off from the spring-fed pool. Follow the trickling water up the side of the mountain. It will eventually lead you to its source and a well deserved soak, well deserved because this is the most strenuous trail to the hot spring. Whichever trail you pick, it is guaranteed to be a nature experience you'll never forget.

JEMEZ SPRINGS

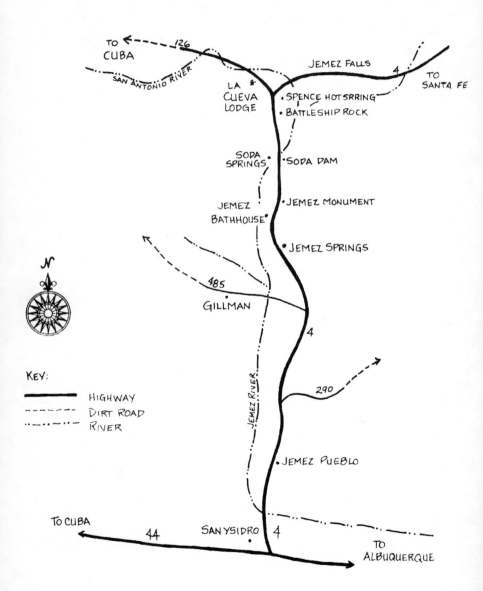

Jemez Springs (Sandoval County)

Location: Located twelve miles north of Jemez Pueblo and two miles south of Soda Dam Springs on Highway 4 in New Mexico.

Elevation: 7500 feet

Temperature: 154°F (68°C)

Flow: 1.3 to 1.9 gpm

Services: The town of Jemez Springs is small but has all necessities available: lodging, food, camping, fishing, exploring, historical monument and a hot spring bathhouse.

The town of Jemez Springs lies in the heart of New Mexico's Indian culture. When the Spaniards first came to Jemez, they found Pueblo Indians already well established in this protected sandstone canyon. This Indian tribe has survived to this very day in the centuries-old village located along the Jemez River. Although you'll find a craft cooperative on the highway, selling the reddish-brown Jemez pottery, a sign warns visitors that no photographs are to be taken without a permit.

Located forty-eight miles northwest of Albuquerque, Jemez Springs is situated in the picturesque Jemez Mountains with red cliffs and blue sky as a backdrop. Another twelve miles up the canyon, just north of the resort village of Jemez Springs, you'll come to a roadside historical marker at the Jemez State Monument. Here you'll find the ruins of a mission church built by the missionaries and Jemez people in the fifteenth century. The marker tells the story:

> The village of Guisewa was occupied by ancestors of the Jemez Indians before the arrival of the Spanish in 1541. Its ruins lie close to those of the great stone mission church of San Jose de Guisewa, which was built by the Franciscans around 1622. Guisewa in Tewa tongue means: place at the boiling waters.

Jemez Springs is the lower of two groups of Springs in the area. Soda Dam (a natural mineral formation, see Soda Dam) is in the upper group. It is said that around the turn of the century there was a hotel at each of these two groups of springs, and stagecoach service brought sophisticated travelers all the way from Albuquerque.

Jemez Springs State Monument.—*Author's Photo*

A gazebo encloses the main spring in the town of Jemez Springs.—
Author's Photo

Jemez Springs Bathhouse

Jemez Springs Bathhouse provides the locals and visitors alike with indoor hot tubs, massage therapy and nice picnic grounds. Both bathhouses in the area have been frequented by visitors from all over the world since the turn of the century. The hot mineral water from the Jemez Spring is said to have therapeutic properties. It has been known to help cure ailments of arthritis, rheumatism, dermatitis and many more.

There's a grocery store nearby. City hall and the ranger station are also located here. And if you're interested, you'll find the old bathhouse behind the Amber Lodge.

A religious cult, that goes by the name Beinzodi, is also present in the area. You can see evidence of their presence as you drive out of town: an austere monastery with huge gardens and robed figures moving silently among secluded buildings.

The Jemez Springs area also offers the visitor the opportunity to ski at Valle Grande in the winter, fish in Fenton Lake, picnic and swim along the rivers and take a hot soak in a private tub at the end of the day.

Soda Dam was formed by the deposit of minerals over the centuries. —*Author's Photo*

Soda Dam Springs (Sandoval County)

Location: Located two miles north of Jemez Springs on Highway 4 on the east side of the highway. Several springs issue here.

Elevation: 6200 feet

Temperature: 115°F (46°C)

Flow: 62 gpm

Services: None.

One of the most popular swimming holes in the Jemez Mountains, Soda Dam is just up the road from the Jemez Springs Resort. There are several hot mineral springs in the area, and Soda Dam is easily the most impressive.

This natural wonder was formed over the centuries by mineral deposits from the flow of thermal springs. In the mid-1960s, the dam was blasted to make way for the highway. This changed the mineral springs' natural course, and ended the build-up of mineral deposits to reinforce the structure. Nonetheless, this is still one of the most spectacular natural formations existing in New Mexico. Who could ask for anything more? A hot spring located in a colorful and breathtaking setting along the Jemez River, below magical mesas of sandstone.

But there's more than just hot springs to keep visitors entertained. The Santa Fe National Forest, of which the Jemez Mountains are the major topographic feature, contain 715,183 acres of wilderness to explore. And the Jemez River, which flows through the Jemez San Diego Canyon, is one of the best fishing streams in the southwest, containing Rainbow, German Brown, and Cutthroat trout.

Farther north you'll find the delights of Fenton Lake, a man-made body of water built by the Department of Game and Fish, which is a refuge for wild fowl. Open year-round, the lake is an excellent place for canoe fishing and has produced trout up to twelve pounds in weight.

Other attractions in the area include the Gilman Tunnels, Red Rocks, Valle Grande and Jemez Falls.

SAN ANTONIO HOT SPRINGS

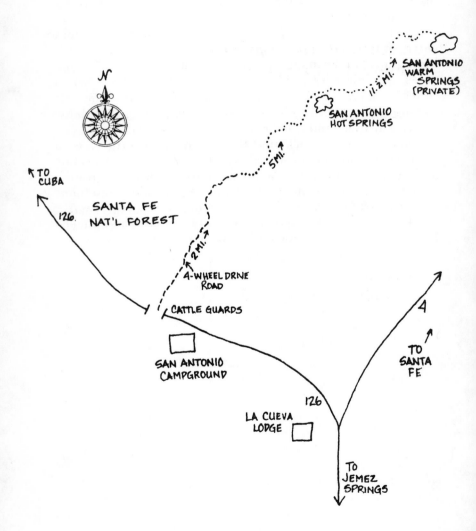

N

SAN ANTONIO
WARM
SPRINGS
(PRIVATE)

11.2 MI.

SAN ANTONIO
HOT SPRINGS

.5 MI.

TO
CUBA

126.

SANTA FE
NAT'L FOREST

.2 MI.

4-WHEEL DRIVE
ROAD

CATTLE GUARDS

4

TO
SANTA
FE

SAN ANTONIO
CAMPGROUND

126

LA CUEVA
LODGE

TO
JEMEZ
SPRINGS

San Antonio Hot Springs
(Sandoval County)

Location: Take Highway 4 north toward Santa Fe, New Mexico then turn off on Highway 128. At this intersection you'll find the La Cueva Lodge and restaurant. Continue past this until you see white cattle guards and a dirt road on the right. This is where you'll begin the trail to the first set of springs in this group. You can drive the dirt road if you have a four-wheel drive. Take this road for about two miles, then park and follow the trail for about four miles. This road is extremely rugged after a rain and winter travel is not advised.

Elevation: 8400 feet

Temperature: 101°F (38°C)

Flow: 199 & 50 gpm

Services: None.

The San Antonio Springs are located in two groups, and will be referred to as San Antonio Hot Spring and San Antonio Warm Spring, hereafter.

San Antonio Hot Spring, also known as Murray Spring, is located in the Santa Fe National Forest approximately six miles from Highway 4 where the trail begins. This spring is situated 250 feet above the San Antonio Creek on the east wall of the San Diego Canyon. It has a flow of 199 gpm and currently provides water for a summer house.

The entrance for San Antonio Hot Springs is marked by a white
cattle guard.—*Courtesy C. Carson*

San Antonio Warm Spring has a small wooden bathhouse built over it.—*Courtesy New Mexico Bureau of Mines and Mineral Resources*

The second spring in this group, San Antonio Warm Spring, is located about four miles north of the first spring along the San Antonio Creek and has a small wooden bathhouse built over it. This spring is located on private property while the first spring is located in the national forest.

Both of these springs have a heavy mineral content and are said to have similar healing properties to Jemez Hot Springs. While these springs are accessible to the public, if you're caught by the local rangers without a permit, they will gladly provide you with a ticket.

SAN YSIDRO
HOT SPRINGS

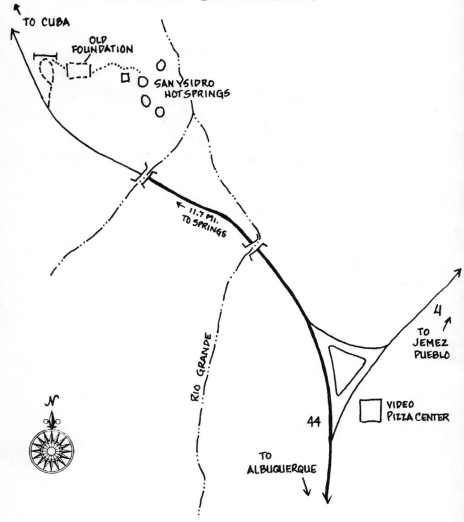

TO CUBA

OLD
FOUNDATION

SAN YSIDRO
HOT SPRINGS

11.7 MI.
TO SPRINGS

RIO GRANDE

4

TO
JEMEZ
PUEBLO

VIDEO
PIZZA CENTER

44

TO
ALBUQUERQUE

N

San Ysidro Hot Springs
(Sandoval County)

Location: Take Highway 4 to intersection of state Highway 44. From the intersection go twelve miles northwest on Highway 44; you'll cross two large bridges. There in the distance you'll see the crumbling foundation of an old building. Hike down from the highway and past the foundation and into a clearing. There are several springs issuing in this area.

Elevation: 7100 feet

Temperature: 85°F (29°C)

Flow: Seep

Services: Nearest services are in the town of San Ysidro.

Although these springs can be difficult to find, there are some forty springs in this area that bubble to the surface along the fault zone of Mesa Blanco. These springs are divided into two groups, those north of Rio Salado and those south.

The springs average about 85°F and there are many craters in the area, some having a diameter of twenty feet and a depth of four feet or more. These geological features suggest the site of extinct thermal springs which had considerably more water in them than the current springs today. This water is not potable for humans, but the range cattle in the area seem to prefer it to the river water.

49

Along Highway 44 hot sulphur springs provide cattle and bathers with naturally hot water.—*Author's Photo*

If you hike down to the springs from the highway, past an old foundation, you'll come to a clearing where there are several shallow rock-lined pools and channels directing the flow of the water. Some of the pools are five to six feet in diameter and approximately two to three feet deep.

If you're a connoisseur of scenery, the color of the landscape will hold your imagination. Shades of red stretch as far as the eye can see. Iron, which naturally occurs in the volcanic areas, oxidizes to create the hues of red. Erosion creates the rest of the artwork.

Spense Hot Springs (Sandoval County)

Location: Located seven miles north of Jemez Springs on Highway 4. The spring issues about one hundred feet above the Jemez River.

Elevation: 8000 feet

Temperature: 102°F (39°C)

Flow: 57 gpm

Services: None.

Two miles north of Battleship Rock picnic area, in between Indian Head and Dark Canyon campgrounds, there's a parking area where the trail to the springs begins.

A well-established path will lead you to the river's edge where fallen timber provides a natural bridge to the other side. From here a steep trail winds through a cool forest and around massive rock outcroppings. About one hundred yards above the river you'll find two rock pools and a wilderness shower. Though the water temperature is hottest at the top pool, it gradually cools as it flows to the lower pool and shower.

This wilderness spring has been used as a natural bathtub for years. In fact, during our visit, a group of loggers came to take the waters at the end of a long day.

It's also a good idea to bring a flashlight with you when you visit the springs. The view is so spectacular and the water so relaxing, you might find yourself staying longer than you had planned. Hot springs sometimes have that effect on people.

A hiker enjoys a wilderness shower at Spence Hot Springs.—
Author's Photo

People come from all over to enjoy the water at Spence Hot
Springs.—*Author's Photo*

Mini waterfalls trickle over rocks and plants.—*Author's Photo*

As you luxuriate in the soothing water, surrounded by nature on all sides, this purifying experience conjures up images of some ancient hedonistic culture.

Note: This is also a nice place to visit in the winter, but the creek can be difficult to cross during the high water season. An alternate log bridge is located about one-half mile upstream.

MONTEZUMA
HOT SPRINGS

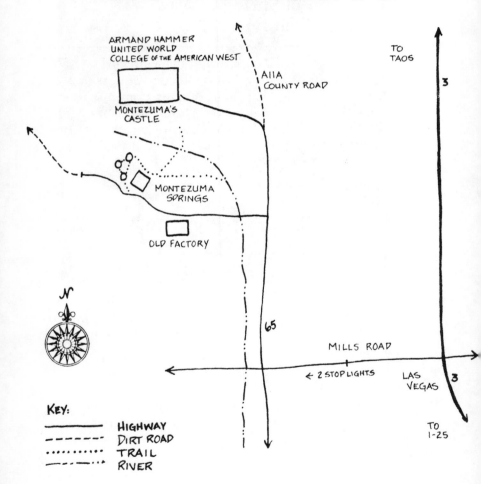

Montezuma Hot Springs
(San Miguel County)

Location: Located on Highway 65 northwest of Las Vegas. From Highway 3 get on Mills Avenue and go two stoplights to Highway 65 and turn right. Continue about five miles to where Highway 65 branches to the west and follow it around. The springs are located off the road on the right.

Elevation: 6400 feet

Temperature: 130°F (106°C)

Flow: 325 gpm

Services: Nearest services are in the town of Las Vegas.

A grand structure overlooks the hot springs. Some call it the Castle, and from a distance it almost looks like a castle, perched there indignantly. As you get closer you can almost feel the history of the place, and images of gothic hotels and mystery novels come to mind.

It was the magic of mineral springs that led to the construction of the hotel. It's sometimes difficult to imagine how five concrete hot tubs, scattered in an open grassy area along the Gallinas River, could have drawn so much attention. Even though the surrounding buildings have been abandoned, the springs are still open to the public.

For centuries the area around Montezuma, New Mexico, has been known for its hot springs which are believed to have curative powers. The fame from these springs led to the construction of several hotels.

In 1841, two brothers, Julian and Anthony Donaldson, were awarded a grant to develop the springs commercially. They failed. Later, the army purchased the springs, believing they would be beneficial to ailing soldiers, and constructed an adobe building to house the ill from nearby Fort Union.

The army sold the hospital in 1862 to O.H. Woodworth who turned it into a hotel. And in 1879, he expanded by building the Hot Springs Hotel next to the old adobe building.

All of this activity peaked the interests of the Santa Fe Railroad, which formed the Las Vegas Hot Springs Company in 1880 and bought the property. The railroad built a grand, 270-room hotel to coincide with the opening of a railroad line into the area. Two years later the huge hotel burned to the ground.

Immediately after the tragedy, the railroad hired famous architects to design and rebuild a new hotel in the Queen Anne style. The Phoenix Hotel cost $300,000 and reopened in April 1885. This new structure was built of red sandstone indigenous to the area, and is the building we see today.

The hotel changed hands many times over the years, until it was purchased by the Armand Hammer United World College of the American West in 1981. Through their efforts to renovate and preserve the 100-year-old Montezuma Hotel, this magnificent castle still survives, though it has been condemned and is not in use.

Left:

Several rustic hot tubs are scattered along the Gallinas River.— *Author's Photo*

The present Montezuma Hotel is home to the Armand Hammer United World College of the West.—*Author's Photo*

TRUTH OR CONSEQUENCES

1. CHARLES BATHHOUSE
2. ROYCE BATHS
3. YUCCA LODGE
4. YE OLD HOT SPRING BATH HAUS
5. INDIAN SPRINGS
6. MARSHALL SPRINGS
7. ARTESIAN MINERAL BATHS

Truth or Consequences
(Sierra County)

Location: Springs located throughout the town.

Elevation: 4200 feet

Temperature: 98°F–114°F (37°C–46°C)

Services: Lodging, grocery store, gas, camping and picnic facilities.

In the beginning the town was called Hot Springs, then in 1950 the name was changed to Truth or Consequences—all because of NBC-TV and radio producer Ralph Edwards. As the story goes, in commemoration of the tenth anniversary of his then renowned radio program, Edwards announced that he wished to find some town in the United States that would like to change its name to "Truth or Consequences." The Hot Springs Chamber of Commerce caught wind of the proposal and the news spread like wildfire. This was a chance to advertise the town and its many natural wonders for free.

A special election was held, and in a landslide vote 1294 citizens favored the change to Truth or Consequences. Only 295 people opposed the change. Of course protests were filed, and the citizens of Truth or Consequences have been to the polls no less than four times over the last few decades to decide the fate of the new name. The outcome is always the same; the name Truth or Consequences has been retained.

Although the name Hot Springs is more indicative of what you are likely to find in the area, the town will never again be obscured among the hundreds of other little towns throughout the United States using the same name Hot Springs. Still there are probably more hot spring establishments per capita in this town than anywhere on earth. Since the days of the Apaches, the springs have been enjoyed for their healing qualities. Today the locals as well as winter visitors enjoy these same springs which flow into the many bathhouses scattered throughout the town.

These are some of the most famous waters of the Southwest. Long before the coming of the white man, the springs were known to native Americans as a place of healing. Indians from all over the continent, traveling many miles on foot, came here to bathe their wounds. Among the most famous of these Indians was Geronimo.

According to local legend, when the Spaniards came they were introduced to the spring by an Indian chief who told them about a huge flat rock that was placed over the main spring, and of the wonderful powers of the magic water it concealed. If some ailment or disease should hit them, or should they have serious wounds, all they had to do was to come and bind the wound with the "White Mud." It was a sure cure. Wounded warriors had long been carried to the hot water, which had the white sand bubbling up. After only two or three baths, they had been known to get up and walk away.

The springs have been used for their medicinal qualities from the beginning, and it is these qualities that have contributed to the growth and development of the community. Eventually the town would become known as a health resort. The springs have been purported to have cured everything from hardening of the arteries to skin diseases.

In the early days, it was believed that if a woman would use this white mud as a face pack, she would become very beautiful in no time. That was said to be the reason for so many beautiful Spanish girls up and down the Rio Grande River. Some still swear by the mud mask.

In those early years the course of the river ran down what is now Main Street as far as the post office. The main part of the city was marsh and swamp. Numerous springs gurgled out of the south hillside with a blanket of white mud extending from the Geronimo Spring, under the post office.

A great deal of credit for the present city should go to Otto Goetz and his family who moved here back in 1913. He was instrumental in obtaining appropriations for the State Bath House, and the beginning of sanitary regulations for bathing places utilizing the hot mineral springs. Goetz helped organize the first chamber of commerce, and all the while operated his own store. He was also instrumental in establishing the first school, and the first city government, and served as mayor of the first village administration.

Today hot spring aficinados will find dozens of bath-houses in Truth or Consequences. Bathers have a range of establishments from which to choose. Here are the most recommended:

Yucca Garden Lodge

316 Austin Street, Truth or Consequences, NM 87901—
1-505-894-3779.

In the center of town, the Yucca Garden Lodge offers lodging and private tubs. Open 7:00 A.M.—7:00 P.M., it is one of the most popular places in town. Here hot spring waters free

Yucca Lodge is the most popular place in town.—*Author's Photo*

flow into three natural pools and one whirlpool where water temperature ranges between 104°F–109°F. Another spring is used for heating the condominiums behind the lodge. There are five rooms, each with its own kitchen, in the main lodge. The minimum stay is three nights.

The lodge has a large circular pool fourteen feet in diameter and four feet deep. Bathing suits are optional in the private rooms. There's also another pool eight feet wide by twenty feet long. The mineral content of the water is: calcium, magnesium, sodium, potassium, bicarbonate, sulphate, chloride, flouride and nitrate silicate.

The current owners have had the lodge for seven years. Reservations are recommended for rooms.

Charles Bathhouse offers a nice place to stay and take in the waters.—*Author's Photo*

Charles Bathhouse and Motel

701 Broadway, Truth or Consequences, NM 87901—
1-505-894-7154.

This 22-room motel has kitchenette, 4 private baths (2 men's and 2 women's), massage therapy during the winter months, beauty shop, gift shop and a wheel chair lift. Temperature: 109°F-111°F. Open all year. Reservations recommended.

The Artesian Bathhouse & Trailer Court offers the visiting RVer the opportunity to enjoy a hot soak and perhaps a massage.—*Author's Photo*

Artesian Bathhouse and Trailer Court

312 Marr Street, Truth or Consequences, NM 87901—
1-505-894-2684

This small RV park offers the visitor hook-ups, 8 private baths, massage therapy and a herbal doctor. Temperature: 101°F-112°F. Open 7:00 A.M.-9:00 P.M. all year. Reservations recommended.

The Marshall Apartments are available on a daily, weekly or monthly basis.—*Author's Photo*

Marshall Apartments

213 S. Pershing, Truth or Consequences, NM 87901—
1-505-894-9948

This small older apartment complex rents by the day or week. It offers spring-fed mineral baths in a private apartment atmosphere. Open all year. Reservations recommended.

Dave's Cloverleaf Baths

207 S. Daniels, Truth or Consequences, NM 87901—
1-505-894-3350.

Massage, acupressure, reflexology and physical therapy is offered at this primarily therapy and health center. Six private tubs.

This hot spring bathhouse offers hot baths, towels are extra.—
Author's Photo

Reflexology is offered at Collins Baths.—*Author's Photo*

Indian Springs Hot Springs Apartments.—*Author's Photo*

Ye Old Hot Spring Bath Haus

205 S. Pershing, Truth or Consequences, NM 87901—

This small establishment offers 5 private baths, but no massage. Temperature: 104°F–108°F. Open daily 7:00 A.M.–10:00 P.M.

Collins Place—Baths

Located on Austin Street.

This small business offers foot reflexology and massage.

Indian Springs Apartments

Located on the corner of Austin and Pershing.

This small complex offers mineral flowing pools in an apartment setting. Daily, weekly and monthly rates. Open all year.

Royce Baths has been a favorite haunt for over fifty years. —*Author's Photo*

Royce Baths

720 Broadway, Truth or Consequences, NM 87901—
1-505-894-3619

This well known bathhouse has been in business for fifty years. Offers private baths, reflexology and massage therapy. Reservations recommended.

Brooks Apartments and Bathhouse

611 Marr, Truth or Consequences, NM 87901—
1-505-894-3431

This older apartment bathhouse offers rooms by daily, weekly or monthly rental.

Ace Lodge

1014 Date Street, Truth or Consequences, NM 87901—
1-505-894-2151.

This older motel bathhouse offers three private tubs. Massage is offered at this establishment.

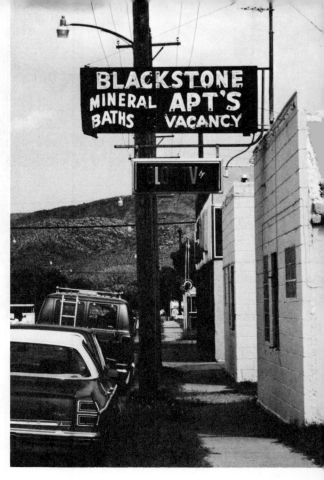

One of the many colorful signs that advertise the bathhouses of Truth or Consequences.—*Author's Photo*

Blackstone Apartments

508 Austin, Truth or Consequences, NM 87901—
1-505-894-6303.

Offers private apartments for rent. Mineral baths. Open all year.

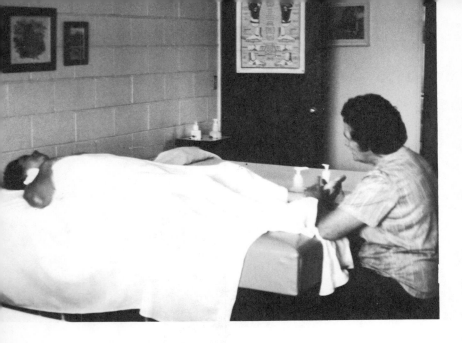

Reflexology or foot massage is offered at many of the establishments throughout the town.—*Author's Photo*

Socorro Hot Springs
(Socorro County)

Location: Located three miles west of the town of Socorro, New Mexico on Highway 60 these springs are private and used by the Geology Department of the New Mexico University just down the hill from them.

Elevation: 5000 feet

Temperature: 91°F (33°C)

Services: None.

Though Socorro Hot Springs is not open to the general public, it is included in this book because the state university at Socorro is the center of most geothermal research in the state of New Mexico.

For more information write:

New Mexico Bureau of Mines & Mineral Resources
Socorro, NM 87801

For geothermal maps write:

U.S. Geological Survey
Denver, CO 80225

or

U.S. Geological Survey
Reston, VA 22092

HONDO/ STAGECOACH HOT SPRINGS

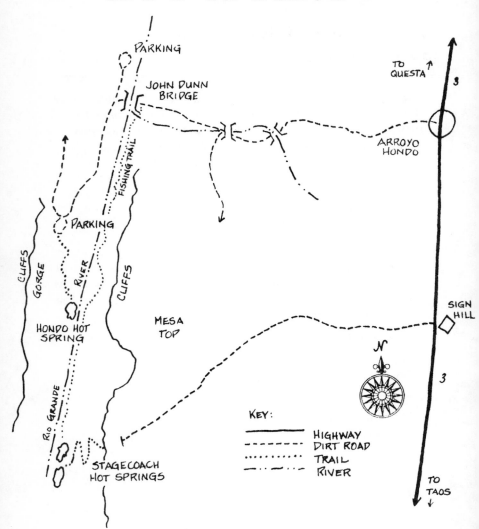

PARKING

JOHN DUNN
BRIDGE

TO
QUESTA

3

ARROYO
HONDO

FISHING TRAIL

PARKING

GORGE

CLIFFS

RIVER

CLIFFS

HONDO HOT
SPRING

MESA
TOP

SIGN
HILL

N

3

RIO GRANDE

STAGECOACH
HOT SPRINGS

Key:

— HIGHWAY
- - - DIRT ROAD
····· TRAIL
— RIVER

TO
TAOS

Hondo/Blackrock Hot Spring (Taos County)

Location: Located north of Taos, New Mexico on Highway 64 in the Hondo-Arroyo area. After crossing the Hondo Bridge, turn left at bar and grocery store onto a dirt road and follow the river. You'll cross the river on a small bridge and go up a rugged hill. When you come to a fork in the road, take the right fork and head up over the mountain and down toward the river. Cross the white bridge, known as the John Dunn Bridge, and continue to the left about one-half mile along the side of the river, climbing until you come to a turnout. You will be on high ground, above the river. The trail starts here at this parking area and can be seen from above.

Elevation: approximately 7000 feet

Temperature: 98°F 37°C)

Flow: unknown

Services: None.

Out in the middle of nowhere, located on the west side of the Rio Grande River in a deep canyon, is a hot spring. When we turned off the main highway in search of this spring, our doubts of ever finding it were high. The only directions we had were incomplete and the gas station attendant wasn't much help either.

Driving slowly on rough dirt roads, we kept our eyes peeled for any signs of hot spring activity. Whenever you're driving and you don't know where you're going it always

Hondo Hot Spring is located along the steep bank of the Rio Grande River.—*Courtesy C. Carson*

seems to take longer. We drove up and down and around for about an hour or so. Finally we drove over the top of a hill and saw the white bridge we were told to cross. Filled with excitement and anticipation, we plodded on to certain success.

We crossed the bridge, turned left, and bounced up a road that was cut into the canyon wall. A steep hike down a hundred yards or more to the edge of the river revealed a secluded mineral pool. Someone had deliberately placed the rocks to allow the cool water from the river to flow into the hot pool. We couldn't have asked for more—a temperature controlled natural hot tub.

Even though our stay at the spring was brief, the surrounding area was so beautiful we knew that we would visit the spring again.

The road to Hondo Hot Spring is a challenge to those searching for New Mexico's remote springs.—*Author's Photo*

OJO CALIENTE MINERAL SPRINGS

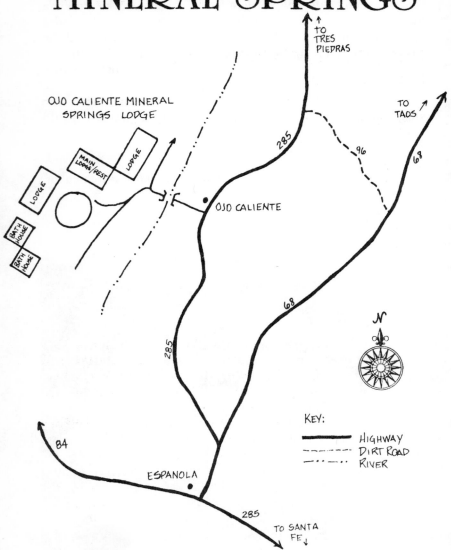

booked

52.00

Ojo Caliente Mineral Springs (Taos County)

Location: Located off Highway 285 just south of Taos, New Mexico, on the outskirts of the small town of Ojo Caliente. One mile north of town in valley of Ojo Caliente Creek. P.O. Box 468, Ojo Caliente, NM 87549—1-505-583-2233.

Elevation: 7200 feet

Temperature: 90°F-122°F (32°C-50°C)

Flow: 350 gpm

Services: Hotel, restaurant, gift shop, bathhouses, pool and recreation facilities.

Super clean, this old hotel has eighteen kitchenettes with TV, and nine motel rooms. The restaurant is cozy and serves a wide variety of dishes including Mexican plates, egg dishes, vegetarian dishes, sandwiches, fruit plates and plans are being made to add even more of a variety.

Breakfast and lunch served 8:00 A.M.-1:00 P.M. and dinner is served from 5:00 P.M.-8:00 P.M.. The hotel offers massage therapy, by appointment only, and sweat wraps.

The original bathhouse and hotel were built in the late 1800s and are now registered with the State Historical Society. There are five springs; all have a different mineral content and purpose.

At the tasting corner, you are encouraged to drink the five different mineral waters which are famous for their curative qualities. A sign explains the benefits of each spring:

Ojo Caliente Hot Springs is registered as a state historic site and is a gourmet bather's delight.—*Author's Photo*

Lithia Spring

Many people feel Lithia relieves depression; aids sluggish kidneys; relieves excess stomach gas.

Iron Spring

We all know that iron is beneficial for the blood.

Arsenic Spring

This wonderful mineral water has been of benefit to those with arthritis; rheumatism; stomach ulcers; promotes relief of burns, exzema and contusions.

Two Soda Springs

These waters are good for over acidic stomach problems.

Another sign is posted:

Use of the Iron Pool is not recommended if you have any skin rash or skin ailment.

78

Legends tell of trails leading to these springs. According to the resort's brochure, in the 1500s, the Spanish explorer, Cabeza de Vaca, described the wonder of his journey to Ojo Caliente as follows:

> The greatest treasure that I found these strange people to possess are some hot springs which burst out at the foot of a mountain that gives evidence of being an active volcano. So powerful are the chemicals in this water that the inhabitants have a belief that they were given to them by their Gods. These springs I have named Ojo Caliente.

Although Ojo Caliente is primarily known as a health resort, hundreds of people come here each year just to rest, relax and to "tune-up" for today's busy schedule. This is an excellent place for a happy-go-lucky vacation.

This is Taos country and there's plenty to see and do in this magical land. History and beauty dominate everything. It's a land of lavender sunsets and old legends about Spanish conquistadores and mountain men.

You might learn a little local history about frontiersmen such as Kit Carson, or you could pay a visit to the shrine of D.H. Lawrence. The ashes of the famous author are kept in a simple adobe building out in the country just outside Taos Pueblo. Art seems to be one of the major industries of the Southwest, and Taos has over eighty galleries where browsing is the most popular pastime.

Not far away, the Rio Grande River runs through a deep gorge, offering the outdoor enthusiast some of the most challenging white water in the state.

North is Taos Ski Valley, known for its spectacular runs down Wheeler Peak, the highest mountain in the state (13,000 feet).

PONCE DE LEON HOT SPRINGS

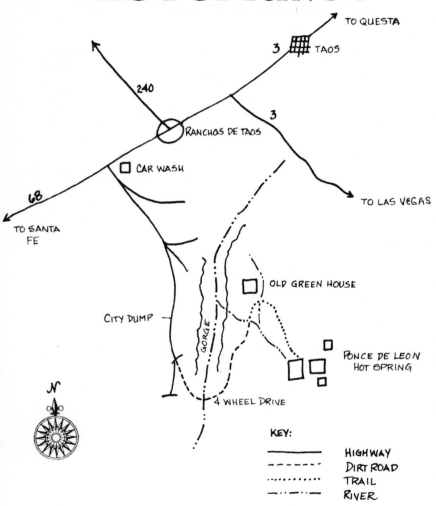

TO QUESTA

3 ⊞ TAOS

240

3

◯ RANCHOS DE TAOS

□ CAR WASH

TO LAS VEGAS

68

TO SANTA FE

□ OLD GREEN HOUSE

CITY DUMP

GORGE

□ PONCE DE LEON HOT SPRING

N

4 WHEEL DRIVE

KEY:

——————— HIGHWAY
– – – – – DIRT ROAD
············· TRAIL
–··–··–·· RIVER

Ponce de Leon Hot Springs
(Taos County)

Location: Located off Highway 68 near the town of Taos. Take the dirt road to the left just after the car wash. The road splits several times; always stay to the right until it becomes too rutted to travel further. Park and walk. Follow the dirt road past the old greenhouse and up the hill. Eventually you'll come to a clearing at the crest of a hill where you'll find one concrete swimming pool and the crumbling remains of another.

Elevation: 6900 feet

Temperature: 95°F (35°C)

Flow: 240 gpm

Services: None.

Ponce de Leon would have been disappointed to see what's become of the hot springs that were affectionately named after him. Only the ruins of a once elaborate resort remain.

In the summer of 1987 we asked in town about Ponce de Leon Hot Springs and were warned that the springs might be closed because someone had drowned out there the previous week.

We decided to go and see what we could find anyway. We followed the directions given to us. Driving a confusing maze of dirt roads, past the city dump, we headed toward the Sangre de Cristo Mountains in the distance. When the road got too rutted we parked the car and walked the rest of the way to the springs.

Natural and concrete pools are filled by hot water springs that once belonged to a resort.—*Author's Photo*

Road leading to Ponce de Leon Hot Springs.—*Author's Photo*

The springs are not isolated, because they are found behind a small pocket of homes, many of which utilized the thermal waters in the area.

At the springs there is a small natural soaking pool (about four feet by five feet) and a larger (twenty-five yard) concrete pool. There is evidence of a huge concrete pool that has had one wall knocked down in order to drain it and discourage bathers after the resort was abandoned years ago.

While the springs are definately off the beaten path, they are not the most impressive springs in New Mexico. But if you're in the area they do merit a visit. Check with local authorities as to the accessibility of the springs.

The surrounding area not only offers two developed ski areas, but also lots of wide open spaces for snowmobiling and cross-country skiing. Summer visitors can fish, hike or just drive around and explore colonial New Mexico. It is an area of Indian pueblos and endless horizons, a land so culturally rich and diverse, you'll never want to leave.

Ruins of an old bathhouse can be found at Stagecoach Hot Springs. —
Courtesy New Mexico Bureau of Mines and Mineral Resources

Stagecoach/Mamby's (American) Hot Spring (Taos County)

Location: Located outside of Taos on Highway 3 near Hondo Arroyo and approximately one and one-half miles south of the John Dunn Bridge at the base of a 600-foot cliff. Water flows about ten feet above river and there is an old bathhouse at the site. See Hondo Hot Spring.

Elevation: 6600 feet

Temperature: 100°F (38°C)

Flow: 30 gpm

Services: None.

This can be a difficult spring to locate. One of the ways to reach it is to drive a dirt road over the top of a high mesa, then scramble down the side of a steep gorge to the river. The other ways are to go by boat or to hike along some of the fishing trails along the river banks until you reach the springs.

River rafters are no strangers to these hot springs, since this is where they beach their baloney boats and make camp near the ruins of the old Santa Fe stagecoach buildings.

This hot spring provides a true wilderness experience. Located on the east side of the Rio Grande River, you'll find two hot springs a few feet above the river. The upper pool will accommodate approximately six people, while the lower pool, which is submerged during high water season, is about the same size.

Minerals and Nutrition

Calcium ....Calcium is needed for bones, teeth,
cartilages, proper blood clotting,
nerve and muscle functioning.

Copper ....Copper is an essential element for
supporting life. In small amounts it is
needed to form hemoglobin.

Flouride ....Flouride has never been proven to be
essential to life, but it is an important
constituent of the elastic fibers of the
skin, the surface of bones and teeth. It
gives hardness and stability.

Iron ....Iron is essential for human nutrition,
since it combines with protein to make
hemoglobin, the coloring matter of red
blood cells. It also aides in the distri-
bution of oxygen through the body.

Magnesium ....Magnesium is needed for the pro-
duction and transfer to energy, muscle
maintenance, protein synthesis, and
many of the chemical reactions in the
body.

Manganese ....Manganese is necessary for bone
development, reproduction,
nerves, and the building and
breakdown of protein cycles in the
body.

Phophorus ....Phosphorus, stored in the bones, is
closely associated with calcium and
vitamin D. Produces energy and builds
new tissue.

Potassium	Potassium is needed for proper muscle function, iron balance, and cell nutrition.
Selenium	Selenium has shown to reduce all types of cancer, helps prevent chromosome breakage. Studies have shown that in communities where selenium intake is low, the cancer rate is high.
Silica	Silica gives strength to bones, nerves, mucous membrane, hair, and nails.
Sodium	A sodium fluid bathes every cell in the body.
Sulfate	Sulphur is found in every cell of the body, but the cells that contain the most sulphur are skin, hair and nails and the fluids in the joints and vertebral discs.
Zinc	Zinc is involved in tissue nutrition and protein building. It is also needed in tissue repair.

Source: Dr. Carl C. Pheiffer, *Zinc and Other Micro-Nutrients* (New Canaan, Conn.: Keats Publishing, Inc., 1978).

Alphabetical Index

Artesian Bathhouse & Trailer Court, 64
Battleship Rock Hot Spring, 35
Brooks Apartments & Bathhouse, 68
Charles Bathhouse, 63
Collins Place, 67
Dave's Cloverleaf Baths, 65
Faywood Hot Spring, 15
Frisco Box Canyon Springs, 7
Gila Hot Spring Center, 19
Hondo/Blackrock Hot Springs, 73
Indian Springs Apartments, 67
Jemez Springs, 39
Lightfeather Hot Spring, 25
Lyons Hunting Lodge Springs, 28
Marshall Apartments, 65
Melanie Hot Spring, 29
Montezuma Hot Springs, 55
Ojo Caliente Hot Springs, 77
Ponce De Leon Hot Springs, 81
Radium Springs, 11
Royce Baths, 68
San Antonio Hot Springs, 45
San Francisco Hot Springs (Lower), 1
San Francisco Hot Springs (Upper), 4
San Ysidro Hot Springs, 45
Socorro Hot Springs, 45
Soda Dam, 42
Spense Hot Springs, 51
Stagecoach Hot Springs, 95
Truth or Consequences, 59
Turkey Creek Hot Springs, 31
Upper Middle Fork Hot Spring, 33
Ye Old Hot Spring Bath Haus, 67
Yucca Garden Lodge, 59

Map Index

Faywood Hot Springs, 14
Frisco Box Canyon Springs, 6
Gila Cliff Dwellings Area, 24
Gila River Basin Area, 18
Hondo/Stagecoach Hot Springs, 72
Hot Springs Diagram, viii
Jemez Springs, 38
Montezuma Hot Springs, 54
New Mexico Hot Springs, iv
Ojo Caliente Mineral Springs, 76
Ponce De Leon Hot Springs, 80
Radium Springs, 10
San Antonio Hot Springs, 44
San Francisco Hot Springs, ivx
San Ysidro Hot Springs, 48
Spense/Battleship Rock Hot Springs, 34
Truth or Consequences, 58
Turkey Creek Spring, 30